CONTENTS

Acknowledgements

The author and publishers wish to thank the following who have kindly given permission for the use of copyright material:

Collins/Harvill Press for extracts from *Into the Whirlwind* by E S Ginzburg;   Constable and Company Ltd. for an extract from *Years Off My Life* by A Gorbatov;   Croom Helm Ltd. for an extract from *Essential Stalin* by Franklin;   Victor Gollancz Ltd. for an extract from *One Day in the Life of Ivan Denisovich* by Alexander Solzhenitsyn;   Granada Publishing Ltd. for an extract from *Stalin* by L Trotsky;   Robert Hale Ltd. for an extract from *I Chose Freedom* by Victor Kravchenko;   M Heath & Co. Ltd. for an extract from *Behind the Urals* by J Scott;   Oxford University Press for extracts from *Memoirs of a Revolutionary 1901–1941* by Victor Serge, translated and edited by Peter Sedgwick (1963); *Endurance and Endeavour: Russian History 1812–1917* by J N Westwood (1973) and *Stalin* by Isaac Deutscher (2nd edition, 1966);   A D Peters & Co. Ltd. on behalf of Ronald Hingley for an extract from *Stalin: Man and Legend*;   Yale University Press for an extract from *Forced Labour in Russia* by Dallin and Nicolaevsky.

The author and publishers wish to acknowledge the following photograph sources:

Archiv Gestenberg pp. 30, 31;   BBC Hulton Picture Library pp. 5, 7, 8, 9 left, 13 top left, 13 bottom, 25.   British Library p. 14;   International Institute voor Social Geschieaems, Amsterdam pp. 22, 23 left;   Novosti Press Agency pp. 9 right, 11 bottom left, 13 top right, 19 top left;   Pictorial Press Ltd p. 11 bottom right;   Popperfoto pp. 18, 19 top right, 38, 45;   Society for Cultural Relations with USSR pp. 10, 11 top, 19 bottom, 23 right, 26;   H. Roger Viollet p. 16.

The publishers have made every effort to trace copyright holders, but if they have inadvertently overlooked any they will be pleased to make the necessary arrangements at the first opportunity.

PREFACE

The study of history is exciting, whether in a good story well told,
mystery solved by the judicious unravelling of clues, or a study of th
men, women and children, whose fears and ambitions, successes an
tragedies make up the collective memory of mankind.

This series aims to reveal this excitement to pupils through a set o
topic books on important historical subjects from the Middle Ages t
the present day. Each book contains four main elements: a narrativ
and descriptive text, lively and relevant illustrations, extracts o
contemporary evidence, and questions for further thought and work
Involvement in these elements should provide an adventure which wil
bring the past to life in the imagination of the pupil.

Each book is also designed to develop the knowledge, skills an
concepts so essential to a pupil's growth. It provides a wide, varyin
introduction to the evidence available on each topic. In handling thi
evidence, pupils will increase their understanding of basic historica
concepts like causation and change, as well as of more advanced idea
like revolution and democracy. In addition, their use of basic study
skills will be complemented by more sophisticated historical skill
such as the detection of bias and the formulation of opinion.

The intended audience for the series is pupils of eleven to sixteer
years: it is expected that the earlier topics will be introduced in th
first three years of secondary school, while the nineteenth and
twentieth century topics are directed towards first examinations.

JOSEPH STALIN

Childhood

Number 10 Cathedral Street, Gori, was less a house than a small, dirty, draughty, two-room shack. The floor of brick chippings was porous enough to absorb some of the pervasive damp; drips from a leaky roof fell into wooden bowls to catch them; there was a smell of wet clothes and cooking; two small four-pane windows near a low door did little to brighten the gloom.

R. Hingley, *Stalin: Man and Legend.*

Here, on 21 December 1879, Joseph Vissarionovich Dzhugashvili was born. In 1912 he was to change his name to Joseph Stalin, Stalin meaning 'man of steel'.

His father, Vissarian, was (according to Hingley) 'a drunken, jack-booted, black-whiskered, bushy-eyebrowed lout' who worked in a shoe factory in the town of Tiflis, sixty-four kilometres from Gori. His mother, Yekaterina, had to supplement the family income by taking in washing, and her dream was that her son should become a priest.

The only first-hand witness who grew up with Stalin was a man named Iremashvili, and from him we learn that, at a young age, Joseph had a very severe attack of smallpox which left his face deeply pitted. Probably as a result of an illness in his youth, his left arm remained permanently a few inches shorter than his right arm. At his birth, the second and third toes of his left foot were joined together.

To understand a little more of Stalin we need to look closely at the Russia in which he became an adult at the turn of the century.

iflis

Russia in 1900

Russia was one of the great world powers and her empire stretche[d] more than 10 000 kilometres, from west to east, from the Arctic waste[s] of Siberia in the north to the sun-baked deserts around the Caspia[n] Sea. In this vast area lived approximately 200 million people, but the[y] were not all Russians. The true Russians lived mainly in the densel[y] populated areas around St Petersburg (later named Leningrad) an[d] Moscow. The rest of the population was made up of small or minorit[y] groups which the Russians had conquered in previous centuries. Suc[h] groups included Poles, Ukrainians and Georgians. Georgia was th[e] area from which Stalin came. These people suffered greatly unde[r] Russian rule and had few rights. They were forced to speak onl[y] Russian, pay heavy taxes to the government, and they had to follo[w] the Russian or Orthodox religion.

At a time when other world powers such as Great Britain, Franc[e] and Germany were growing as great industrial and agricultur[al] nations, Russia remained a very backward nation. Approximately 98[%] of its population were peasants who worked the land and who ha[d] been slaves, owned by wealthy noblemen, until 1861. In the citie[s] lived factory workers. As we shall see in a later chapter, they live[d] lives of great misery.

The ruler of this empire was known as the Tsar. He ruled Russia a[s] an autocrat – meaning that he alone had total power to make laws. I[n] 1900 the tsar was Nicholas II. He was a loving family man to his wif[e] and five children but, as his ministers remarked, he was 'unfit to run [a] village post office'. They also said that 'the last person to see Nichola[s] made up his mind for him'. He was a weak ruler who did not full[y] understand Russia's problems. Encouraged by his wife, Alexandr[a] his main concern was to hold on to complete power so that he coul[d] pass the crown on to his son.

There was so much discontent in Russia at this time that there gre[w] up a number of revolutionary groups, dedicated to overthrowing th[e] Tsar and his family. One of these groups was a small band of abou[t] eight men led by Gregory Plekhanov. They called themselves th[e] Social Democrats, or the Russian Marxists.

Marxism

This group followed the teachings of Karl Marx, a German journalis[t] who in 1848 had published a book called *The Communist Manifesto*. A[s] a result he had been expelled from his country. He fled to England[,] died in 1883 and is buried in Highgate Cemetery, in London. In th[e] *Manifesto* and other books he divided the world into two:

1 *The bourgeoisie* who owned the country's wealth, ran her industrie[s] and ruled, and
2 *The proletariat* or workers who led lives of great unhappiness an[d] poverty, controlled as they were by the bourgeoisie.

Marx's solution

He maintained that this situation would continue for ever unless the workers grouped together, rose in revolution and overthrew their rulers. The *Manifesto* ended with the words, 'Let the governing classes tremble before the Communist Revolution. The proletariat have nothing to lose but their chains. They have a world to win. Workers of the world, unite!' Marx predicted that when the revolution had been achieved,

1 the workers would rule their country
2 the workers' government would take over all industries, banks, transport and land
3 all people would have a right to be educated, and
4 all people would be equal.

Stalin's education

In 1898, at the age of nineteen, Stalin joined the Marxist group in Tbilisi. He was familiar with the many problems of Russia. His parents had themselves been peasants, he lived and worked amongst the industrial workers, and he belonged to a minority group, the Georgians.

His mother had sent him to Tbilisi in 1894, to a school or seminary which trained young men for the priesthood. He hated it. He later wrote:

I became a Marxist because of my social position . . . but also . . . because of the harsh intolerance and Jesuitical discipline that crushed me so mercilessly at the Seminary. . . . The atmosphere in which I lived was saturated with hatred against Tsarist oppression.

His teachers also were suspicious of him. The conduct book at his seminary contains a number of accounts showing Joseph's increasingly poor behaviour. One such report reads, 'Dzhugashvili is generally disrespectful and rude towards persons in authority and systematically refuses to bow to one of the masters'. In 1899 the school expelled him. Because of his involvement with the Marxists, he was to spend the next seventeen years in and out of prison.

A prison officer later wrote about Stalin:

Once, I remember, I had to order him to be flogged. I had no alternative for he had been preaching rebellion to the other prisoners, and the punishment for that was clearly laid down in orders. As commanding officer, I had to attend the punishment, though it was a duty I always hated. He presented himself – reading one of his books. The blows fell. He continued to read. The senior warder ordered him to lay down his book, but he merely went on reading. The book was torn from his hand and thrown to the floor, and the last lashes laid on.

...alin, a student at the
...minary in Tbilisi

7

Row 1: | бр. виду 37 | рост. 1 метр 74 | сант. | Раса (если цветнокожий) | |

	Перенос. (глуб.)			Выс. врх. губ.		„Волн."		Лоби.-нос. ч.
	Спинка	Осиов.		Вист.		„Особ."		Нижн. ч. лиц.
	Высота	Вист. 1	„Шир."	Борадр.		Накл.		Выс. череп.
				Толщин.		Высота		Особ.

He neither winced nor cried out, though they were savage enough. And when it was all over and his hands were freed, he stooped down, picked up his book, resumed reading as though what had happened had been merely a trivial interruption.

Stalin 1900–17

Although Stalin spent many of these years in prison, he also gradua grew to be a more important member of the Marxist group in Russ

Stalin the prisoner

1 Imprisoned in 1903, 1908, 1910, 1912. Escapes three times

2 World War I breaks out in 1914. In 1917 Stalin rejected as medically unfit for the army

3 1917 Imprisoned again

Stalin the revolutionary

1 In between prison, organis bank robberies to obta money for the Marxists

2 1903 Becomes a Bolshev (see below)

3 1905 Meets Lenin for the fi time

4 1912 Lenin makes him member of the Bolshev Central Committee

5 1917 Lenin makes Stal editor of the Bolshevik new paper *Pravda* (meaning 't truth')

Stalin, Lenin and the Bolsheviks

By the beginning of the twentieth century, quarrels were breaking out between the Russian Marxists. They had been joined by a young man, Vladimir Ulyanov, who called himself Lenin. He and Plekhanov, the leader of the group, argued over how a revolution should be carried out in Russia.

Plekhanov	*Lenin*
All the people should rise	The rising should be carried out by a small, dedicated group of men
↓	↓
Overthrow the Tsar	Overthrow the Tsar
↓	↓
Set up a new government run on Marx's ideas	Set up a new government run on Marx's ideas

In 1903 a significant meeting was held by forty-four Marxists who had been thrown out of Russia, and then were moved on by the police from their rat-infested warehouse in Belgium. They came to London, and after many bitter arguments about these two sets of ideas a vote was taken.

Result: Plekhanov's supporters: 21 votes
              Lenin's supporters: 23 votes

In recognition of this result Lenin called his group the *Bolsheviks* or majority party. Plekhanov's group became the *Mensheviks* or minority party. Stalin read Lenin's ideas and became one of his most dedicated followers. Stalin wrote of him:

> *In Lenin we had a man of extraordinary calibre. I did not regard him as a mere leader of the Party, but as its actual founder, for he alone understood the inner essence and urgent needs of our Party. . . . Lenin was the mountain eagle of our Party.*

enin died in 1924
bove   *A mourner at
enin's funeral. It was so
old that his moustache
roze*

ight   *The embalmed body
f Lenin*

1917–27

Lenin returned to Russia in 1917, and in October he achieved what seemed impossible; his Bolshevik party seized control of the key cities of Russia. The Tsar became a prisoner of the Bolsheviks. In July 1918, the Tsar and his family disappeared. Stalin had played no part in the revolution, as he was still a prisoner. But on his release he quickly became a key figure amongst the Bolsheviks. Lenin died in 1924, and by 1927 Stalin had become the party leader, in control of the whole USSR, overpowering his closest rival, Trotsky.

USSR Russia, in 1923, was renamed the Union of Soviet Socialist Republics

Questions
The Stalin legend

1 Study the picture of Stalin as a boy. It is a painting that Stalin commissioned of himself.
  a) When do you think this picture was painted?
  b) What is Stalin trying to show in the painting?

Stalin, the schoolboy, is the one leading the group, holding his cap

10

Study the picture of Stalin with Lenin at a meeting in July 1917
a)   Where do you think the meeting may have occurred?
b)   Where, in fact, was Stalin at this time? (Refer back to page 8).
c)   When, why, and by whom, do you think the picture was painted?

Study the photographs of Stalin below.
a)   How is he made to appear a popular and heroic figure?
b)   How is his air of authority and leadership created?
c)   Which of Stalin's physical defects are disguised?

In all these photographs Stalin was encouraging the growth of a 'personality cult'.
a)   What do you think is meant by this?
b)   By what other methods could a personality cult be encouraged?

Stalin with Lenin at a meeting in 1917

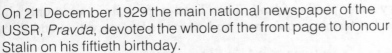

alin congratulating the wives of Red Army commanders in 1937

New Year's Fir Tree Party

On 21 December 1929 the main national newspaper of the USSR, *Pravda*, devoted the whole of the front page to honour Stalin on his fiftieth birthday.
Imagine that one of the articles had the headline: 'Stalin's rise to power'. Write your own paragraph on what this would say.

11

2 | STALIN AND AGRICULTURE

In 1931, Stalin made a speech to the first Conference of Workers fro
all over the USSR. He said:

> *The history of the old Russia has consisted in being beaten again and
> again because she was backward. She was beaten by Mongol Khans,
> beaten by Turkish beys, beaten by Swedish Feudalists. She was
> beaten by Polish-Lithuanian gentry. She was beaten by Anglo-
> French capitalists. She was beaten by Japanese barons. All have
> beaten her because of her backwardness; military backwardness . . .
> industrial backwardness, agricultural backwardness. She was beaten
> because to beat her has paid off and because people have been able to
> get away with it. . . . If you are backward and weak, then you are in
> the wrong and may be beaten and enslaved. But if you are powerful
> . . . people must beware of you.*
>
> *We are fifty to a hundred years behind the advanced countries. We
> must make up this gap in ten years. Either we do this or they crush us.*

Beys   Turkish rulers

Stalin was right: the USSR was a very backward country in bo
industry and agriculture in the 1920s. In this speech, Stalin show
his determination to increase both food and industrial production
make the USSR as powerful as other nations.

Russian peasants

The peasants were the largest class of people in the USSR, and th
were divided into four groups:

Kulaks: The richest peasants who owned land, rented it to othe
and hired extra workers.

Seredniaks and *Muzhuks:*   They had enough land to support ther
selves, but did not hire more labour.

Bedniaks: Poor peasants with small plots who, to earn extra mone
worked on Kulak land.

Batraks: Had no land and earned a wage by hiring themselves out
labourers.

The majority of these peasants, with the exception of the Kulaks, h
very small pieces of land. They lived in poor huts, used only simp
wooden farming equipment and were used to starvation and diseas

They were satisfied if they could provide enough food for their ow
families and perhaps sell off a little surplus to provide extras like sa

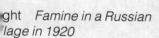

or fuel. The one-roomed shacks into which the family had to crowd
were often shared with animals. Food in the winter was often in such
short supply that animals were fed thatch from the roofs of the huts.

Karl Marx had said that when the revolution happened, the
government should take land from private owners. Between 1918 and
1922 Lenin had tried to seize the peasants' land and set up large
state-controlled farms, but he had met with great resistance from the
peasants. As he and his party were still fighting to control the USSR
he gave way to the peasants, allowing them to keep their land and
to continue to sell off any surplus produce.

Stalin would not tolerate this. He wanted large amounts of grain
and food to feed the growing towns, and he wanted to make the USSR
self-sufficient. In 1929 not enough grain was produced and there was a
serious bread shortage. Stalin said:

13

We are beginning seriously to re-equip agriculture. For this we must expand the development of collective and state farms, *employ on a mass scale the contract system and machine and tractor stations as a means of establishing a bond between industry and agriculture along the lines of production. As for the present grain-purchasing difficulties, we must admit the necessity for temporary emergency measures.* We must reinforce the support of the middle and poor peasant masses, as one of the means of breaking the resistance of the Kulaks *and of obtaining from them the maximum grain surplus. This is necessary in order to be able to dispense with importing grain and to save foreign currency for the development of industry.*

The words that are not in italics summarise Stalin's agricultur policy, which was:

1 to set up collective farms
2 to destroy the Kulaks who were likely to oppose this. He plann to destroy them with the help of the less fortunate peasants.

Collective farms *(known as Kolkhoz)*

Here is how they were to function:

Peasants
↓
Hand over most of their land to the Kolkhoz
↓
Kolkhoz managed by a committee elected by the local Communist Party
↓
Kolkhoz set an annual production target by Stalin

In this cartoon, the complacent Kulak with his fertile plot (in the background) was intended to arouse jealously and hatred towards wealthy farmers among the ordinary peasants

КРОКОДИЛ

Distribution of the Kolkhoz's production

15%   had to be given to the government at a fixed low price.

5%   had to be given to the government at a higher price.

15%   had to be given to the machine tractor station which supplied each collective with the machinery it needed.

40%   was used to buy seeds, etc.

25%   was distributed amongst the peasants as wages.

Each member of the Kolkhoz was allowed to keep a small vegetable garden, a few tools, their home and a few animals.

Resistance of the Kulaks

As predicted, the richer peasants hated the idea of the collective and from 1929 to 1933 put up great resistance. The novelist Mikhail Sholokhov wrote:

> *Animals were slaughtered every night. Hardly had dusk fallen than the muffled bleats of sheep, the death squeals of pigs and the lowing of calves could be heard. Both those who had joined the collective farm and individual farmers slaughtered their stock. 'Slaughter, they'll take it for meat anyway.... Slaughter, you won't get meat on the collective farm ...' crept the rumours. And they slaughtered. They ate till they could eat no more. young and old suffered from indigestion. At dinner-time tables groaned under boiled and roasted meat. At dinner-time everyone had a greasy mouth, everyone hic-coughed as if at a wake. Everyone blinked like an owl, as if drunk from eating.*

Here are some figures to show the slaughter between 1929 and 1933.

16 out of 34 million horses slaughtered

30 out of 60 million cattle

100 million sheep and goats.

The Kulaks burnt and destroyed their land and homes and hid their grain rather than hand it over to the collective.

What Stalin did

1   He first organised groups to hunt out and seize the peasants' grain. Then he let the peasants starve. Victor Kravchenko, a Communist, wrote about a village in the Ukraine in 1932 to which he had been sent:

> *We arrived at the large village of Petrovo towards evening. An unearthly silence prevailed.*
>
> *'All the dogs have been eaten, that's why it's so quiet,' the peasant ... said.*

Famine victims

'I will not tell you about the dead,' [a villager] said. 'I'm sure you know. The half-dead, the nearly-dead are even worse. There are hundreds of people in Petrovo bloated with hunger. I don't know how many die every day. Many are so weak that they no longer come out of their houses.

'A wagon goes around now and then to pick up the corpses. We've eaten everything we could lay our hands on – cats, dogs, the field mice, birds. When it's light tomorrow you will see that the trees have been stripped of their bark, for that too has been eaten. And the horse manure has been eaten!'

I must have looked startled and unbelieving.

'Yes, the horse manure. We fight over it. Sometimes there are whole grains in it.'

2 Secondly, Stalin began the threatened elimination of the Kulaks. Kravchenko again wrote about a village that he visited:

A large crowd was gathered outside the building. Policemen tried to scatter them, but they came back. A number of women and children were weeping hysterically and calling the names of their husbands and fathers. It was like a scene in a nightmare....

In the background, guarded by the soldiers with drawn revolvers, stood about twenty peasants, young and old, with bundles on their backs.... I saw two militiamen leading a middle-aged peasant. It was obvious that he had been manhandled – his face was black and blue and his gait was painful; his clothes were ripped in a way indicating a struggle.

These peasants were sent to the labour camps.

3 You will read about these camps in a later chapter. Victor Serge, a Russian journalist, wrote of them:

Trainloads of deported peasants left for the icy north, the forests, the steppes, the deserts. These were the whole populations, denuded of everything; the old folk starved to death in mid-journey, new-born babies were buried on the banks of the roadside, and each wilderness had its crop of little crosses of boughs or white wood.

It is difficult to know how many Kulaks died; estimates have varied from 13 to 30 million. About three million died from starvation in 1932–3.

For and against the Kolkhoz: the big debate
Against: In 1929 an American returned to his village in Central Russia and described his visit to the home of Yekim:

The huge coarse table was laden with cucumbers, bread, empty wooden dishes, spoons, round which flocks of flies buzzed viciously. His wife came in with a pail of fresh milk. She strained it into two earthen jars.... Neighbours had begun to gather. They had heard of my arrival and they stopped in on their way home from the fields, sickles on their shoulders, wooden water-buckets on their backs. They were bursting with eagerness to talk – and their chief topic was the Kolkhoz.

'There was a time,' began Lukyan who had been a blacksmith, 'when we were neighbours. Now we are Bedniaks, Seredniaks, Kulaks. I am a Seredniak, Boris here is a Bedniak and Nisko is a Kulak and we are supposed to have a class war....

'But it is other things that worry us ... whoever heard of such a thing – to give up our land and our cows and our horses and our tools and our farm buildings, to work all the time and divide everything with others? Nowadays members of the same family get in each other's way and quarrel and fight, and here we, strangers, are supposed to be like one family. Can we make it "go" without scratching each other's faces, pulling each other's hair or hurling stones at one another? ...'

'We won't even be sure,' someone else continued the lament, 'of having enough bread to eat. Now however poor we may be, we have our own rye and our own potatoes and our own cucumbers and our own milk. We know we won't starve. But in the Kolkhoz, no more potatoes of our own, no more anything of our own. Everything will be rationed out by orders; we will be like mere Batraks on the landlord's estates in the old days. Serfdom [slavery] – that's what it is – and who wants to be a serf?'

'Yes, and some women will have ten children and will get milk for all of them; another will have only one child and will get milk for only one and both will be doing the same work. Where is the justice?'

Above   *Two girls showing the 1932 and 1933 grain harvest of their village*

Below   *A sowing machine on the Kolkhoz*

For: The organiser of the Kolkhoz arrived and joined in the discussion:

'*I suppose they have been shedding tears about the Kolkhoz,*' he said....

'*Tell me, you wretched people, what hope is there for you if you remain on individual pieces of land? From year to year as you increase in population you divide and sub-divide your strips of land. You cannot even use machinery on your land because no machine man ever made could stand the rough ridges that the strip system creates. You will have to work in your own way and stew in your old misery. Don't you see that under your present system there is nothing ahead of you but ruin and starvation?*

'*You accuse us of making false promises ... last year you got a schoolhouse, and have you forgotten how we of the Party and of the Soviet had to squeeze out of you through the voluntary tax your share of the cost of the schoolhouse? And now? Aren't you glad your children can attend school? ... Were we wrong when we urged you to build a fire station? Were we wrong when we urged you to lay decent bridges across your stream in the swamp? Were we wrong when we threatened to fire you if you didn't take home two loads of peat to mix with the bedding for your stock so as to have good fertiliser?*' ...

'*The Kolkhoz is different,*' shouted the old man.... '*Of course it is different. If we didn't believe in making things different, we never would have overthrown the Tsar and the capitalists and the landlords.... Different? Of course, but better.*

'Don't you see? Isn't it about time you stopped thinking each one for himself and for his own piggish hide? You Kulaks of course will never become reconciled to a new order. You love to fatten on other people's blood. But we know how to deal with you. We'll wipe you off the face of the earth.'

above   The first electric bulb is lit in a Russian village 1928

right   Threshing on the kolkhoz

below   A collective farm with its own sanitorium

Questions

1 Make a list of all the reasons why the Kulaks were opposed to collective farms.
2 Give the reasons why the organiser thought they were necessary.
3 Study the photographs produced by Stalin's government.
  a) Write down all the ways in which they show that collective farms improved agriculture and the lives of the peasants.
  b) To what extent would these photographs be biased?
4 Study the tables given below.

Livestock numbers 1916–63 (in million head)

	1916	1928	1938	1940	1945	1950	1955	1959	196
Cattle	59	67	51	55	48	57	67	74	8
Pigs	20	28	26	28	11	24	52	53	4
Sheep and goats	115	115	87	92	70	99	143	144	14
Horses	35	36	—	21	11	14	14	11	9

Grain harvest 1913–70 (in millions of tonnes)

1913	1928	1940	1945	1960	1970
76	69	75	47	125	167

  a) What conclusions do you draw from the results of collectivisation in the period
    (i) 1928–38?
    (ii) 1945–63?
  b) Why was there such a slump from 1940–45?
  c) Taking all the evidence that you have studied in this chapter, would you say that collectivisation improved Soviet agriculture output or not?
  d) Using the 'big debate' evidence and the photographs, do you think that Stalin's agricultural policy helped the Russian peasant or not? Give reasons for your answer.

STALIN AND INDUSTRY

The USSR has great mineral wealth, in particular coal, iron ore and oil. Yet in 1913 she was far behind Britain and the USA in industrial development. Here are some figures for that year:

USSR coal production: $\frac{1}{10}$ of that of GB
$\frac{1}{17}$ of that of the USA
USSR oil production: $\frac{1}{3}$ of that of the USA
USSR steel production: $\frac{1}{2}$ of that of GB
$\frac{1}{8}$ of that of the USA

Not only was the USSR not developing its natural resources but over 33 per cent of her industry was in the hands of foreigners, in particular France, Germany, Britain, Belgium and the USA. Stalin was determined to change this situation, to make the USSR into a great industrial power.

Why was this necessary? Industry was needed:

1 to supply the population with fuel, textiles and necessary consumer goods
2 to produce weapons for the armed forces
3 to manufacture exports which could bring hard currency into the country
4 to supply agriculture with machinery and equipment.

Lenin's legacy

From Lenin, Stalin inherited a depressed industrial scene. Years of war — first the World War of 1914–18, then civil war from 1918 to 1922 — meant that many areas of industry had almost come to a standstill. Railway track had either been torn up or abandoned, and although much of Russian industry was now nationalised or controlled by the government, a proportion was still in the hands of private ownership. In 1921 Lenin had created the State Planning Commission, or GOSPLAN, whose task was to plan the expansion of Soviet industry. Stalin took over GOSPLAN, and in 1928 it produced, under his direction, the first five-year plans.

The five-year plans

Stalin stressed that output had to increase by 300 per cent if Russia was to compete with other countries. From 1928 to 1933 targets were

ЭТО-ЖИВЫЕ ЛЮДИ, ЛЮ МЫ ВА
(с

ШЕСТЬ УСЛОВИЙ ПОБЕДЫ

1. Организованно набирать ра-
   бочую силу
2. Уничтожить уравниловку
3. Ликвидировать обезличку
4. Создать свою собственную

производственно - техниче-
скую интеллигенцию
5. Больше внимания к «старым
   специалистам
6. Укрепить хозрасчет

ШИРОКОЕ РАЗВЕРТЫВАНИЕ СЕТИ
ЯСЛЕЙ, ДЕТСКИХ САДОВ, СТОЛОВЫХ
И ПРАЧЕШНЫХ ОБЕСПЕЧИТ
УЧАСТИЕ ЖЕНЩИНЫ
в СОЦИАЛИСТИ
ЧЕСКОМ СТРО
ИТЕЛЬСТВЕ

ПЯТИЛЕТ-
НИЙ
ПЛАН
1928 г.

ФАНТАЗИЯ
БРЕД
УТОПИЯ

This 1931 poster says that more nurseries, laundries and canteens will mean that women can take part in the industrial growth

In 1928 a gloating rich man calls the 5 year plan 'a fantastic dram'. In 1933 he is angry at being proved wrong

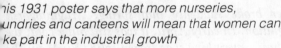

left   In the centre, Stalin is urging his workers to move forward with him towards industrial growth

set for the following industries: coal, iron, chemicals, steel, machinery. Coal output had to rise from 35 million tonnes to 75 million tonnes, oil from 12 million to 22 million tonnes. Six times as much electricity was to be produced. Posters such as these were displayed to urge workers to work harder.

Magnitogorsk

Let us take one town in the Ural Mountains, Magnitogorsk. The map shows you its location and the main centres of heavy industry.

Magnitogorsk had a population of 1 157 people in 1929, living in tumble-down houses with unpaved streets and open sewers. Four years later it had a population of over 100 000, together with mills, blast furnaces, shops, a school and a hospital, as a result of Stalin's five-year plan. Where did all these workers come from? Many were young people, filled with enthusiasm by the persuasive publicity to flock to the industrial centres. Figures for 1933 show that about 45 000 came of their own free will, another 18 000 were recruited, but 50 000

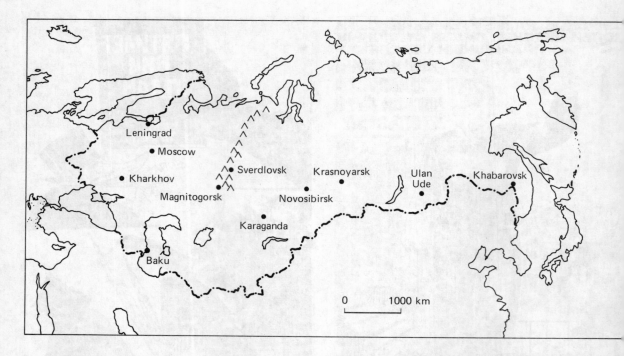

Main centres of heavy industry in Russia

were forced labourers who were made to do all the heavy work such a digging foundations and wheeling concrete. We know that th number was mainly made up of Kulaks and political prisioners. Th conditions were horrific. One British engineer, John Scott, wh worked in Magnitogorsk wrote:

As the Arctic winter broke suddenly into spring, Magnitogorsk changed beyond recognition. In early April, it was still bitter cold, we had hardly a single thaw, everything was frozen solid. By May, the ground had thawed and the city was swimming in mud ... welding became next to impossible as our ragged cables short-circuited at every step.... Bubonic plague had broken out in three places not far from Magnitogorsk....

The resistance of the population was very low because of under-nourishment during the winter and consistent overwork. Sanitary conditions, particularly during the thaw, were appalling....

Within two weeks the sun was upon us. By the middle of May the heat was intolerable. In the barracks we were consumed by bed-bugs and other vermin, and at work we had trouble keeping to the job.

Despite these conditions, some workers managed to produce almos superhuman efforts. Alexis Stakhanov, in 1935, produced 102 tonne of coal in one six-hour shift and began what was known as th Stakhanovite movement. Those who followed his example wer rewarded with cash prizes, holidays and medals; but there were man others who were crushed under the enormous burden of work. Stri measures were brought in against these supposed 'slackers'. The included:

The targets of the first 5 year plan are displayed on this machine placed in the centre of the town

1 Punishment for absence. Even if a worker was twenty minutes late this was counted as an absence. A second absence meant a jail sentence.

2 The working day was increased to eight hours, and everyone had to work six days out of seven.

3 School leavers were sent without choice to areas where there was a labour shortage.

4 Any worker found slacking or any manager not fulfilling the target was sent to a labour camp.

5 All workers carried labour books which showed their jobs, their qualifications and any offences they had committed.

Some problems and results of industrialisation

Some of the problems that workers faced in 1928–33 have already been listed in John Scott's account. There were others.

Problems

1 *The enormous influx of new peasant workers in the First plan raised many problems. Despite emergency measures, it was impossible to train them properly so that much inefficiency, as well as accidents to people and machinery, resulted. The peasant was unused to factory discipline. By tradition he tended to slacken his effort as soon as his earnings covered his necessities; after a certain point he preferred leisure to money. . . . He was used to working hard and long at certain seasons and taking things easy at other times and this attitude was transferred to industry. . . . The new worker did not always realise that work could go on when it rained, or that punctuality was essential. . . . In these years it was typical for workers to change their jobs four or five times a year, making it difficult to train them.*

J.N. Westwood, *Endurance and Endeavour: Russian History 1812–1917*, published in 1973

2 a) *It was a varied gang, Russians, Ukrainians, Tartars, Mongols, Jews, mostly young and almost all peasants of yesterday, though a few, like Ivanov, had long industrial experience. . . . On the other hand, Khaibulin, the Tartar, had never seen a staircase, a locomotive or an electric light until he had come to Magnitogorsk a year before. . . . Now Khaibulin was building a blast furnace bigger than any in Europe. . . .*

b) *The scaffold was coated with about an inch of ice, like everything else around the furnaces. . . . But besides being slippery, it was very insecure, swung down on wires, without any ropes to steady it. It swayed and shook as I walked on it. . . . I was just going to start welding when I heard someone, and something swished past me. It was a rigger who had been working at the very top. . . .*

John Scott

25

3 *In the course of 1928–31, wrecking organisations (saboteurs) were
discovered in the following industries: coal-mining, defence, textiles,
machinery, chemical, rubber, oil, in transport and in the retail trade.*

I. Trifanov, a Russian economist

Results

1 Study the photographs of Sverdlovsk before and after the five-year
plan, thinking about the differences that they show.

*Sverdlovsk in the Ural
Mountains in 1928*

Sverdlovsk in 1933

2 *In 1938 though the city [of Magnitogorsk] was still in a primitive state ... it did boast 50 schools, 3 colleges, 2 large theatres, half a dozen small ones, 17 libraries, 22 clubs, 18 clinics.... A large park had been constructed in 1935....*

The city of Magnitogorsk grew and developed from the dirty, chaotic construction camp of the early thirties into a reasonably healthy and habitable city. A street car line was constructed and went into operation. New stores were built and supplies of all kinds made their appearance in quantity and at reasonable prices. Fuel, clothing of all kinds, and other elementary necessities became available. It was no longer necessary to steal in order to live.

John Scott

3 Study the table.

Russian Economic Growth 1913–65
(figures in million tonnes)

	1913	1928	1940	1945	1950	1960	1965
Iron ore	9	6	30	–	40	106	153
Steel	4	4	18	12	27	65	91
Coal	29	36	166	149	261	513	578
Oil	9	12	31	19	38	148	243

Questions

1 Read all the extracts on the problems of industrialisation, and make a list of the key problems.
2 What do the tables and the photographs tell you about the success of Stalin's industrialisation programme?
3 How do the industrial statistics compare with those of agriculture?
4 'Stalin's industrial policy was a success, but it was achieved at the expense of human suffering.' Do you agree with this opinion? Give reasons for your answers.

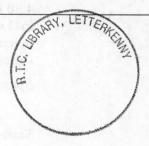

4

THE GREAT PURGE, 1936~9

Arrest

I went out in the cold morning in Kazan to do some shopping. I am aware of being followed, which is quite natural. Except that by this time 'they' are trailing so close behind me that I begin to be worried. As I come out of the chemist's shop they stop me. This is on the pavement of the October 25th Prospect, with everybody bustling past all around me. 'Criminal Investigation. Kindly follow us, citizen, for purposes of identification.'

So wrote Victor Serge, a poet, of his arrest just before Stalin's Great Purge swept through the USSR. Serge was lucky, for although he was moved to five different prisons, questioned, searched and sent to a labour camp, he survived. Thousands did not.

The Great Purge

What exactly was the Great Purge? It was the period from 1936 to 1939 when millions of Russian people (politicians, doctors, writers, generals, peasants, industrial workers, people from every walk of life) were arrested by Stalin's agents. Some were put on trial, but many were not. Without trial they could be sent to the horrific labour camps of Siberia, or simply executed. Their relatives often never heard of their fate. Fear became a part of everyday living – fear of the knock on the door in the middle of the night, fear of the tap on the shoulder. Women lost their husbands, sisters and sons; children their fathers, mothers and friends, for in 1935 Stalin decreed that even twelve-year-olds could be executed. Schools encouraged their pupils to spy on and denounce their parents as enemies of the state.

The event which began the Purge was the assassination of Sergei Kirov, chairman of the Leningrad Soviet. On 1 December 1934, at 4.30 in the afternoon, he entered the corridor of the Smolny Institute in Leningrad and was shot dead. Stalin immediately ordered an investigation into the murder, and suspicion fell on two of Trotsky's closest friends, Kamenev and Zinoviev. Then events moved quickly.

Spring 1935	Thousands of people living in Leningrad were imprisoned or shot because Stalin claimed they were conspirators in Kirov's assassination.
Summer 1936	Zinoviev, Kamenev and fourteen others were charged with Kirov's death and were executed.

1937	Marshal Tukhachevsky, the Soviet Union's most distinguished soldier, together with seven generals, was executed without trial for 'espionage and treason to the Fatherland'.
1938	Yagoda, head of the secret police or NKVD was executed. He had been tortured and made a startling confession to having murdered his predecessor, assisting in Kirov's murder, admitting foreign spies into the NKVD and even planning a military coup together with the assassination of the whole Politburo!
1938	In this year, it is estimated that over a fifth of the Communist Party were expelled or shot following the notorious 'Moscow trials'. This number included leading officials, secretaries to the Party, Komsomol members, industrial managers, foreign Communists, writers, scholars, engineers and scientists.

Interrogation

One woman, Eugenia Ginzburg, a lecturer, wrote about her arrest and interrogation by the NKVD in 1937:

> *The interrogators worked in shifts; I didn't. Seven days without food or sleep, without even returning to my cell. . . . The object of the 'conveyor' is to wear out the nerves, weaken the body, break resistance, and force the prisoner to sign whatever is required.*
>
> *The first day or two I still noticed the individual characteristics of the interrogators – Livanov, calm and bureaucratic as before, urging me to sign some monstrous piece of rubbish. . . . Tsarevsky and Vevers always shouting and threatening – Vevers sniffing cocaine and giggling as well as shouting. . . . Major Elshin was invariably courteous and 'humane'. He liked talking about my children. He asked me why 'I was becomingly pale' and was 'amazed' to hear that I had been questioned without food or sleep for four or five days. . . .*

Interrogators were instructed to use every form of physical pressure and violence to get their victims to sign confession documents. The prisoners were kept in solitary confinement during and after interrogation. Victor Serge describes his cell in Moscow's dreaded Lubianka Prison, which still exists today:

> *The cell was bare with only a bed, table and chair. . . . On the freshly painted walls there was not a single scribble or scratch. . . . Here, in absolute secrecy, with no communication with any other person, with no reading-matter, with no paper, with no occupation of any kind, with no open-air exercise in the yard, I spent about eighty days. It was a severe test of nerves. My diet, consisting of black bread with wheaten or millet batter and fish soup, meant I had hunger pains every day.*

29

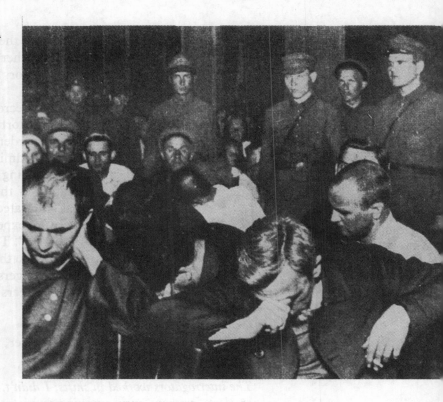

Show trials

Many of Stalin's victims were never put on trial but simply shot or imprisoned. However, prominent public figures were given 'show trials' as an example and warning to the Soviet people. The most famous of these show trials was the Trial of the 16, held in August 1936. The sixteen accused included Zinoviev, Kamenev and fourteen others accused of plotting the murder of Stalin and Kirov. Vyshinsky was the main prosecutor. Eventually all sixteen broke down and confessed to the charges against them, were found guilty and shot. Many others, often innocent people, suffered the same fate. Why did so many confess? Ronald Hingley in his book on Stalin writes:

> They were held in isolation for months or even years on end, deprived of sleep, periodically harangued, cajoled or browbeaten night and day by frenzied tormentors ... but in many cases such extreme methods were not even necessary, for threats and promises – affecting the victims' families as well as themselves – were often sufficient.

The Purge outside Russia

Even some of those Russians living in the West did not escape Stalin's henchmen. Many died in mysterious circumstances. The most famous death perpetrated by Stalin was that of Trotsky, living in Mexico. Trotsky knew that Stalin wanted to liquidate him so he had his villa fortified with steel doors, machine gunners and electric alarm systems. The first attempt on his life came in May 1940, when a team of

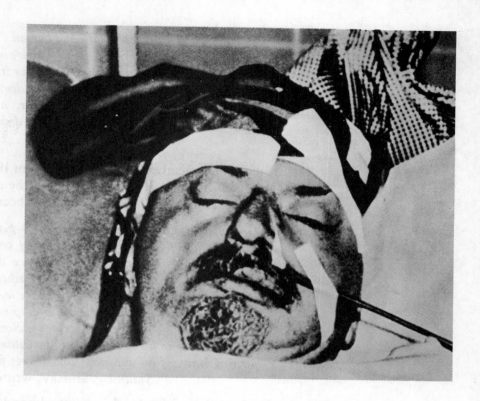

assassins burst into his villa riddling Trotsky's bedroom with seventy-three bullets. Miraculously, Trotsky and his wife escaped, but in August 1940 a young Spanish Stalinist, Ramon Mercader, succeeded in breaking in and smashing Trotsky's skull with an ice-axe. The blood covered the papers on which Trotsky was writing. They were part of a book on Stalin.

The Purge ends
Stalin finally brought the slaughter to an end in 1938, when he made Beria head of the NKVD. It is impossible to obtain accurate figures for the number of victims claimed by the Purge, but one estimate is that about three-quarters of a million were shot and between seven and fourteen million sent to the labour camps.

Why did the Great Purge happen?
The verdict of one historian, Ronald Hingley, is that Stalin's subjects were persecuted 'on a scale greater than that caused by any other ruler in history – [with] suffering, degradation and death'. Was Stalin, therefore, simply a sadistic monster? We need to make our judgements from the evidence available to us: from those who knew him, from Stalin himself and from historians writing after his death.

1 *He [Stalin] is unhappy at not being able to convince everyone, himself included, that he is greater than everyone else; and this unhappiness of his may be his most human trait, perhaps the only*

31

human trait in him. But what is not human . . . is that because of this unhappiness he cannot avoid taking revenge on people. . . . If someone speaks better than he does, that man is for it! Stalin will not let him live, because that man is a constant reminder that he, Stalin, is not the first and the best. . . . No, no, Fyodor, he is a narrow-minded, malicious man – no, not a man, but a devil.

Bukharin

Bukharin, a member of the Politburo from 1918 to 1929, was execute by Stalin in 1938. He was speaking in the extract to Fyodor Dan Paris in 1936. Dan, a Menshevik, had been deported in 1922.

2 *Undoubtedly characteristic of Stalin is personal physical cruelty, which is usually called sadism. During confinement in the Baku prison, Stalin's cell neighbour was once dreaming of revolution. 'Have you a craving for blood?' Stalin asked him unexpectedly. He took out a knife that he had hidden in the leg of his boot, raised high one of his trouser-legs and inflicted a deep gash on himself. 'There's blood for you!' After he had become a Soviet dignitary, he would amuse himself in his country home, by cutting the throats of sheep or pouring kerosene on ant-heaps and setting fire to them.*

Stalin by Trotsky, written in Mexico in 1939.

3 (a) *It was right after Kirov's murder in 1934 that Beria began to climb to prominence and power. . . . His influence on my father grew and grew and never ceased until the day of my father's death. . . . Beria was more treacherous, more practised in perfidy and cunning, more insolent and single-minded than my father. In a word, he was a stronger character. My father had his weaker sides. He was capable of self-doubt. He was cruder and more direct than Beria and not so suspicious. He was simpler and could be led up the garden path by someone of Beria's craftiness. . . . The spell cast by this terrifying evil genius on my father was extremely powerful and it never failed to work.*

Svetlana Alliluyeva, Stalin's daughter (1963)

(b) This letter, quoted in Svetlana's memoirs, was written by Stali to his daughter between 1930 and 1932:

You don't write to your little papa, I think you have forgotten him. How is your health? You're not sick, are you? What are you up to? How are your dolls? I thought I'd be getting an order from you soon, but no. Too bad. You're hurting your little papa's feelings. Never mind. I kiss you. I am waiting to hear from you.

Little Papa

Extracts 3(a) and (b) are taken from the memoirs of Stalin's daughte written in 1963. She was born in 1926, so during the Purges she wou have been 10–12 years old.

cartoon published in Paris
y those who had fled
talin's Russia. It shows
talin dominating the
overnment

4 Stalin said, 'Well, go on, Svetlana, dance! You're the hostess, so dance!'

She said, 'I've already danced, Papa, I'm tired'. With that, Stalin grabbed her by the forelock of her hair with his fist and pulled. I could see her face turning red and tears welling up in her eyes. I felt so sorry for Svetlana. He pulled harder and dragged her back onto the dance floor. . . . His behaviour toward her was really an expression of affection, but in a perverse, brutish form which was peculiar to him.

Khruschev (who succeeded Stalin after his death in 1953)

It is not clear when this was written, but it was probably after Khruschev's fall from power in 1964.

5 (a) But why did Stalin need the abominable spectacle [of the Purge]? It has been suggested that he sent the men of the old guard to their death as scapegoats for his economic failures. There is a grain of truth in this, but not more. For one thing, there was a very marked improvement in the economic condition of the country in the years of the Purge. Stalin's real and much wider motive was to destroy the men who represented the potentiality of alternative government, perhaps not of one but of several governments.

33

(b) *The opposition was pulverised, downtrodden, incapable of action. Only some shock, some convulsive disorder involving the whole machinery of power, might have enabled it to rally its scattered and disheartened troops. A danger of that kind was just then taking shape and it threatened from abroad. The first of the trials, that of Zinoviev and Kamenev, took place a few months after Hitler's army had marched into the Rhineland; the last, that of Bukharin and Rykov, ended to the accompaniment of the trumpets that announced the Nazi occupation of Austria.*

Isaac Deutscher, historian: *Stalin*, 1966

6 *There was a popular theory for the purges in the prisons – the labour force theory. It explained the countless arrests as due to the need for manpower in remote areas, where people refused to go. . . . It did not explain why the workers on such great projects were called enemies of the state. . . .*

Ian L. Carmichael, historian: *Stalin's masterpiece*

7 *In 1937, new facts came to light regarding the fiendish crimes of the Bukharin-Trotsky gang. . . . The trials showed that these dregs of humanity . . . enemies of the people . . . had been in conspiracy against Lenin, the Party and the Soviet State ever since the early days of the October Socialist Revolution. . . . The trials brought to light the fact that the Trotsky fiends, in obedience to the wishes of their masters – the espionage services of foreign states – had set out to destroy the Party and the Soviet state, to undermine the defensive power of the country, to assist foreign military intervention, to prepare the way for the defeat of the Red Army, to bring about the dismemberment of the USSR, to hand over the Soviet Maritime Region to the Japanese, Soviet Byelorussia to the Poles, and the Soviet Ukraine to the Germans, to destroy the gains of the workers and collective farmers and to restore capitalist slavery in the USSR. . . . These contemptible lackeys of the fascists forgot that the Soviet people had only to move a finger, and not a trace of them would be left. The Soviet court sentenced the Trotsky fiends to be shot. The People's Commissariat of Internal Affairs [the NKVD] carried out the sentence. The Soviet people approved their annihilation and passed on to the next business.*

Stalin: *A Short History of the Communist Party*, 1938
(This book was used in Russian schools.)

8 *By exterminating without any mercy these spies, provocateurs, wreckers and diversionists, the Soviet land will move even more rapidly along the Stalinist route, Socialist culture will flourish even more richly, the life of the Soviet people will become even more joyous.*

Pravda (the newspaper of the Russian Communist Party)
10 March 1938

VISITEZ L'U.R.S.S.
SES PYRAMIDES!...

e caption for this cartoon
ads: 'Visit the USSR's
yramids!...' The shape is
rmed by the skulls of those
ho died in the Purges

Questions

1 Using the first-hand accounts by Bukharin, Trotsky, Svetlana and Khruschev, make a summary of Stalin's personality, saying:
   a) How the extracts agree
   b) How they differ
   c) Are there any reasons to doubt the accuracy of each?
2 What motives for the Purges are suggested by the historians Deutscher and Carmichael? Does Stalin's account agree with them in any way?
3 What evidence is there in Stalin's account and that of *Pravda* of propaganda about the Purges?
4 You are writing a history of Stalin's Russia. Write a paragraph to explain why the Purges occurred.

5

THE LABOUR CAMPS

*The Kolyma region is a desolate land at the very edge of the world, in
the coldest wastes of the Arctic. Its rivers are ice-bound 8 to 9 months
a year, and the continuous polar night covers it for 6 to 8 weeks in the
winter. When a blizzard sweeps over the land, usually lasting for
several days, even the hardened inhabitants never go out without first
tying themselves to their cabins with a rope. In the blinding gale they
might never find their way back and might lose their lives within a few
steps of their homes. The temperature of the region sometimes drops to
−92°F so that mercury becomes as malleable as lead and iron as
brittle as glass.*

Dallin and Nicolaevsky: *Forced Labour in Russia*

This region is in the north-eastern tip of the Soviet Union, and even in
the summer the sun's heat can only thaw out the very top layer of soil
turning it into a swamp. Below this, the ground remains permanently
frozen. Many insects are attracted to the area during the short weeks
of warmth, especially mosquitoes and huge gadflies whose sting can
pierce a deer's hide.

A census in 1926 showed that the region had a population density of
one or two persons to every two kilometres or so. It was then chosen as
one of the areas for Stalin's labour camps, and its population grew
from a few Arctic tribesmen to about two million prisoners. The
prisoners made up a rhyme about the region:

*Kolyma, wonderful planet,
Twelve months winter, the rest summer!*

Perhaps the best way to portray the true horror of these labour camps
is to look at the case histories of four prisoners and their accounts of
the conditions they had to suffer.

Case History 1   Alexander Gorbatov

Gorbatov was known as a distinguished general in the 1930s, but
during Stalin's purge of the Red Army in 1937–8 Gorbatov was
arrested. He was first interrogated in a Moscow prison, left 'bloody
and exhausted', then transferred to another prison, further tortured,
before being transferred to a labour camp. This is his story.

The Camp   *The camp, surrounded by barbed wire, contained ten
big hospital-type double tents for fifty to sixty prisoners each. There
were also wooden buildings, containing a mess hall, storehouses and a
guard room. Outside the wire were wooden barracks for the guards
and also two gold mines and two drums for washing the dirt.*

Prisoners *In our camp there were about 400 men, political prisoners, and up to fifty urkagans or hardened criminals who had on their consciences more than one conviction, some several and others even as many as eight robberies with violence. It was from among these that the seniors were appointed.*

Work a) *The dirt was extracted from a depth of 35 to 40 metres. Since permafrost is a solid, granite-like mass, we used miners' electric drills. The dirt we removed was carried in barrows to a special hoist, lifted up the shaft to the surface and then delivered to the washing drums in small trucks.*

Work at the mine was quite exhausting, especially in view of the bad food. As a rule, the hardest work was given to the 'enemies of the people' (the political prisoners) and the lightest to the 'friends' or urkagans.

b) Gorbatov was transferred to a second camp.

This was a large hutted camp at the foot of the mountains. We dragged huge loads of wood a day, four kilometres down the mountain. It will be difficult for readers to imagine the scene as along the mountain slopes in a file four kilometres long emaciated men, not men but shadows, dragged the wood along, summoning up the last of their strength, their heads bent forward like migrating cranes.

Food *The food came in three categories; for those who had not fulfilled their norms, for those who had and for those who had overfilled them. The urkagans were among the latter. Although they worked very little, the tally clerks were from among their number and they swindled us and attributed our output to themselves. Thus the criminals had their fill and we starved.*

Result By the end of his three-year sentence:

I had grown extremely thin; my height is 177 centimetres but at the time I weighed only 64 kilograms. The only sign that I was a military man was my tunic, which had served me continuously through these years. It was difficult to determine what its colour had been through the dirt and patches. My wadded trousers were in patches. My feet were wrapped in footcloths. . . . I also had a quilted jacket shiny with dirt. On my head I wore a tattered and dirty hat with earflaps. In my pocket I had my emergency kit – ten small crackers and five pieces of broken loaf sugar.

In 1941 Gorbatov was released because Stalin needed him to lead Russian troops in World War II. His career continued until 1954 by which time Stalin had decorated him with many honours.

Case History 2 Eugenia Ginzburg
Eugenia was a Communist, living in Moscow in the 1930s. During this

time she worked for a historian whom Stalin accused of being a Trotsky supporter. Eugenia was also suspected, arrested and separated from her husband and two young children. Her children were transferred to other towns and given different names. She was tortured, interrogated and given a ten-year sentence. The first year she spent in solitary confinement, and in the third year she was transported to her first labour camp.

Camp a) *The camp consisted of a huge, dirty yard surrounded by barbed wire; it stank intolerably of ammonia and chloride of lime which was for ever being poured down the latrines. A special breed of bugs infested the long wooden huts. Already gorged with the blood of our predecessors, they no longer crawled but moved swiftly, impudently, purposefully, in large groups.*

b) She stayed in this camp for a few months and then was transported by ship to another camp. She describes her journey there:

At last we reached the hold, a greasy place of tangible stuffiness. Packed tightly in our hundreds we could hardly breathe. . . . When I opened my eyes I saw rows of faces with bloodshot eyes and pale dirty cheeks. There was a sickly acrid smell. The sea was fairly calm; nevertheless the weaker among us were sea-sick. They vomited over their neighbours and over our greasy bundles. For the first time I met with lice . . . fat white creatures which crawled peacefully around.

Food *The food contained no vitamins whatsoever. For breakfast we got bread, hot water and two lumps of sugar; for dinner soup and gruel cooked without any fat and for supper, a kind of broth reeking of fish oil.*

Work She writes that their work was called 'land improvement'. *Before dawn we were marched to a bleak open field. Until 1 p.m. we hacked at the frozen soil with spades. We ate between 1 p.m. and 1.30 at the camp, trying to warm ourselves over the stove. From 1.30 p.m. until 8 p.m. we worked again.*

Punishment Because the women were so weak, they could only produce 18 per cent of their target output. For this they were punished by being locked in a special punishment cell and put on a starvation diet.

We lived in a shack resembling a public lavatory. We were not allowed out of it to attend to our natural needs and no bucket was provided. At night we had to take turns on the three logs provided that served as bunks, so most of the time we had to sleep standing up. In the morning we were again driven out, wet and hungry. . . .

Results Eugenia described the effects of living in labour camps on one prisoner that she met, Tanya Stankovskaya:

I realised that she was not a girl but an old woman with dishevelled grey hair and dry scaly skin on her bony face.... 'How old was she?' 'Thirty-five,' she said. 'That surprises you doesn't it?' She had spent three years as a prisoner....

She was ghastly to look at. Her skin was peeling more and more and her teeth had grown long and irregular and stuck out between her chapped lips like the palings of an old fence. She still said nothing about her ills, but everyone could tell she was having frightful diarrhoea. Twenty times a day she climbed down from the bunk, grey, dishevelled, terrifying – clattered in her over-sized boots to the corner of the room where in place of the prison slop-pail a big hole gaped in the floor.

Tanya was diagnosed to have scurvy, a disease brought about through lack of vitamins in the diet. Her death followed a few months later.

She was carried to the camp and placed on a bench from which she never rose again.... To add to her suffering she had become blind and could only hold my hand....

In 1955 Eugenia Ginzberg was released, two years after Stalin's death. By then she had spent eighteen years as a prisoner. She was never to see her husband or eldest son again.

Case History 3 Maria Joffe

She was a journalist who in 1929 protested against Trotsky's expulsion from the country. She was arrested, sent to prison, kept in solitary confinement and then transported to labour camps where she was kept from 1929 to 1957. Her one son was a young child when she was sentenced.

Prostitution To gain extra food, a number of women prisoners became prostitutes. Maria writes of one called Mashka:

She stood one hand on her hip and a rolled cigarette in the other, looking like a painted scarecrow amidst the grey-coated prison world. She wore boots with soft, creased, turned-down tops, bright blue cotton slacks loosely tucked into her boots and over it all, a crumpled cotton dress brightly printed with a design of bunches of red flowers.... The hem of the dress was tucked into her belt showing a slip with torn seams underneath. Her hair was done in curlers made of many-coloured rags and she wore great brass ear-rings.

Camp Routine *Reveille. 'One step out of line and I will fire.' Work, thin prison soup and roll call. We work 10 hours a day, walking to the quarry or forest and back, sometimes five to six kilometres and this in your own so-called 'rest time'.*

Punishment She was placed in the 'special isolator' in solitary confinement. Here is her description of the cell:

It was one metre in width and less than two in length. An enormous latrine bucket without a cover and almost overflowing even before my arrival stood in front of me with strings of wood lice over it and the walls. The floor was covered in human excrement . . . there was no air whatsoever, none, only unbearable stench stifling my throat. Breakfast was bread and a mug of very hot water to wash in and drink. . . .

Result Maria Joffe was released in 1957, by which time her 17-year-old son had been 'liquidated'. Her flat was continuously bugged and searched until she received permission from the authorities to leave Russia. She now lives in Israel.

Case History 4 Alexander Solzhenitsyn
Alexander Solzhenitsyn was arrested in 1945 for having made remarks against Stalin. He spent the next eight years in labour camps, some 'general camps' for political and general criminals, and some years in the harder 'special camps'. These extracts, based on his experiences in camps, are from his book *One Day in the Life of Ivan Denisovich.*

Food a) *The prisoners sat in the cold mess-hall, eating slowly, picking out putrid little fish from under the leaves of boiled, black cabbage and spitting the bones on the table.*
b) *The skilly [a thin gruel] was the same every day. Its composition depended on the kind of vegetable provided that winter. Nothing but salted carrots last year. This year it was black cabbage. In July, they shredded nettles into the pot.*
c) *Without neglecting a single fish scale or particle of flesh on the brittle skeleton, Shukhov went on champing his teeth and sucking the bones. He ate everything – the gills, the tail, the eyes when they were still in their sockets, but not when they'd been boiled out and floated in the bowl separately. Not then. The others laughed at him for that.*
d) *After the skilly, there was majara porridge. It had grown cold too and had set into a solid lump. He broke it up into pieces.*
e) *He hides a piece of black bread by sewing it into his mattress. The bread is removed when Denisovich is alone. Then nibbling the bread bit by bit, working the crumbs up into a paste with his tongue and sucking it into his cheeks. How good it tasted, that soggy bread.*

The Cold a) *The cold stung. A murky fog wrapped itself around them and made them cough. The temperature out there was −27°. The prisoners, now clad in all their rags, a cord around their wrists, their faces bound from chin to eyes with bits of cloth against the cold, waiting with leaden hearts for the order, 'Out you get'.*
b) *In the huts – mattress and grubby blanket, head on pillow stuffed with shavings of wood, feet in jacket sleeve, coat on top of blanket. No one ever took off his wadded trousers at night or you'd grow numb with cold.*

Result Alexander Solzhenitsyn was released in 1953 when Stalin died. He now lives in the USA.

Camp death rate taken from *The Great Terror* by Robert Conquest, a historian. Figures for 1937–38:

      Arrested   7 000 000
Died in camp   2 000 000

Camp Illnesses taken from information supplied by the prisoners themselves:

scurvy	dysentery
night-blindness	frostbite
mental derangement	gangrene
syphilis	pneumonia

Camp work taken from Robert Conquest's book. Figures for 1941:

		Prisoners involved
1	Mining	1 000 000
2	Agriculture	200 000
3	Lumbering	400 000
4	Government work, e.g. railway building	1 000 000
5	Camp construction and maintenance	600 000
6	General construction	3 500 000

Questions: *Where should the labour camps be built?*
1 Draw up a list of reasons for choosing a particular site for a labour camp.
2 Study the map which shows the vegetation regions of Russia, and make a chart showing which site would be preferred.

Site   *Order of preference*
A
B
C
D
E

3 You are an NKVD agent sent to write a report on the best site to which prisoners can be sent. Give a full account of why you chose this particular site.
4 The case histories and pictures all show the horror of the labour camps. Why do you think it is so difficult to find evidence to support the government's view of this period?
5 Are there any reasons that Stalin himself might have given to defend the building of such camps?

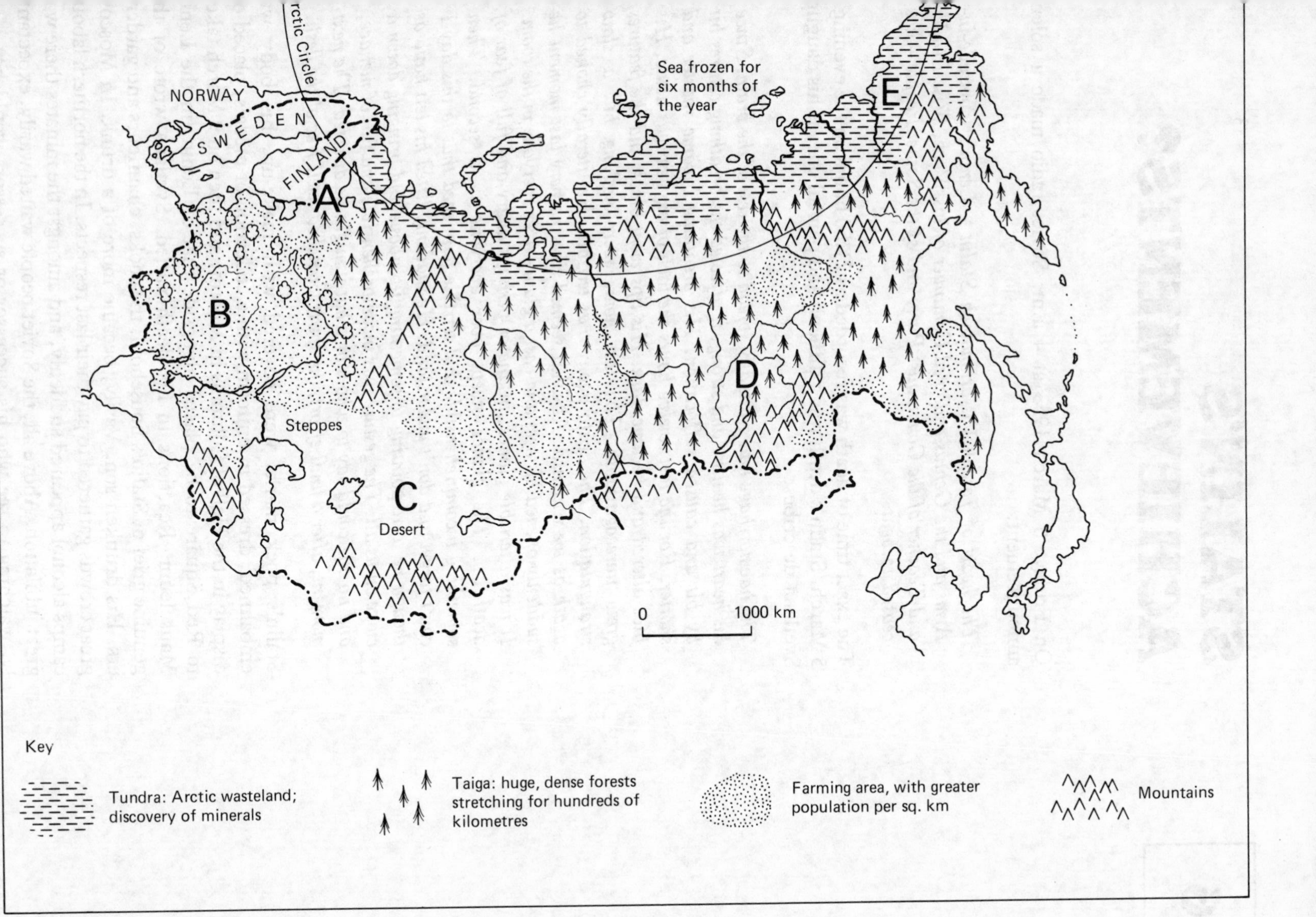

Vegetation regions of Russia

Key

Tundra: Arctic wasteland; discovery of minerals

Taiga: huge, dense forests stretching for hundreds of kilometres

Farming area, with greater population per sq. km

Mountains

Sea frozen for six months of the year

Arctic Circle

NORWAY

SWEDEN

FINLAND

A

B

C
Desert

Steppes

D

E

0   1000 km

6

STALIN'S ACHIEVEMENTS?

On Friday, 6 March 1953 at 4 a.m. Soviet radio made a solem announcement:

> *The heart of Joseph Vissarionovich Stalin – Lenin's Comrade-in-Arms and the Genius-endowed Continuer of his Work, Wise Leader and Teacher of the Communist Party and of the Soviet People – has ceased to beat.*

The exact time of death was recorded as 21.50 hours on the evening 5 March. Stalin's death was a difficult and painful one, as his daught Svetlana describes:

> *The haemorrhage had gradually spread to the rest of the brain. Since his heart was healthy and strong, it affected the breathing centres bit by bit and caused suffocation. His breathing became shorter and shorter. For the last twelve hours the lack of oxygen was acute. His face altered and became dark. His lips went black and the features grew unrecognisable. The last hours were nothing but a slow strangulation. The death agony was terrible. He literally choked to death as we watched. At what seemed like the very last moment he suddenly opened his eyes and cast a glance over everyone in the room. It was a terrible glance, insane or perhaps angry and full of fear of death.... The glance swept over everyone in a second. Then something incomprehensible and terrible happened that to this day I can't forget and don't understand. He suddenly lifted his left hand as though he were pointing to something up above and bringing down a curse on us all. The gesture was incomprehensible and full of menace, and no one could say to whom or what it might be directed. The next moment, after a final effort, the spirit wrenched itself free of the flesh.*

Stalin's pock marks were covered with make-up, his body wa embalmed, dressed in uniform with a collection of medals, placed o display in the Hall of Columns in Moscow and then on 9 March take to Red Square to be placed alongside that of Lenin, in the Leni Mausoleum. Reactions to his death varied. Svetlana wrote of th genuine grief of Stalin's household: the cooks, chauffeurs and garden ers. His drunken son, Vasily, became more of a drunk. In Mosco great crowds gathered to pay their last respects. In the northern labou camps alcohol appeared suddenly, and amongst the inmates there wa great jubilation. Above all, the Soviet people waited warily, expectant ly, watching to see who his successor or successors would be.

talin lying in state

The successor who emerged was Nikita Khruschev. In 1956 he began what was publicly known as a de-Stalinisation programme, opening with a speech denouncing Stalin (part of which you will read later in this chapter). On 31 October 1961 Stalin's body was removed from the mausoleum and cremated; the ashes were buried below the Kremlin wall. A plain slab of black granite was erected bearing a simple inscription:

J.V. Stalin 1879–1953

Only in 1970 was this replaced with a large sculpture of his head and shoulders, resting on a stone plinth.

Stalin: an assessment

Since Stalin's death, much has been written about him. Interpretations vary from those who consider him to be a murderer who did much damage to his country, to those who regard him as a hero. Your final task is to look at the evidence and then make your own judgement.

1 *Svetlana Alliluyeva*

a) This extract is taken from *20 Letters to a Friend*, the book she wrote in 1963 and which was published in 1967 after she had left Russia. She writes of her grief at her father's death:

They know that I was a bad daughter and that my father had been a bad father, but he had loved me all the same, as I loved him.

No one in this room looked on him as a god or a superman, a genius or a demon. They loved and respected him for the most ordinary human qualities, those qualities of which servants are the best judges of all.

b) Her next book, *Only One Year*, was published in 1969 after she had lived in the USA for 12 months. This is how she wrote about her father:

He gave his name to this bloodbath of absolute dictatorship. He knew what he was doing. He was neither insane nor misled. With cold calculation he cemented his own power, afraid of losing it more than anything else in the world. And so his first concentrated drive had been the liquidation of his enemies and rivals. The rest followed later.

2   *Nikita Khruschev's* speech given to the 20th Congress of the USSR in 1956. He compares Lenin and Stalin:

During Lenin's life the Central Committee of the Party was a real expression of collective leadership of the Party and the nation. . . . Lenin never imposed by force his views upon his co-workers. He tried to convince; he patiently explained his opinions to others.

Stalin acted not through persuasion, explanation and patient co-operation with people but by imposing his concepts and demanding absolute submission to his opinion. Whoever opposed this concept or tried to prove his viewpoint was doomed to removal.

3   *Bruce Franklin,* an American university lecturer who became a Communist in 1965, wrote in 1973 in support of Stalin:

The Soviet Union of the early 1920s was a land of deprivation. Hunger was everywhere, and actual mass famines swept across much of the countryside. Industrial production was extremely low, and the technological level of industry was so backward that there seemed little possibility of mechanizing agriculture. Serious rebellions in the armed forces were breaking out, most notably at the Kronstadt garrison in 1921. By 1924 large-scale peasant revolts were erupting, particularly in Georgia. There was virtually no electricity outside the large cities. Agriculture was based on tiny peasant holdings and medium-sized farms seized by rural capitalists (the Kulaks) who forced the peasants back into wage labour and tenant farming. Health care was almost non-existent in much of the country. The technical knowledge and skills needed to develop modern industry, agriculture, health and education were concentrated in the hands of a few, mostly opposed to socialism, while the vast majority of the population were illiterate and could hardly think about education while barely managing to subsist.

When Stalin died in 1953, the Soviet Union was the second greatest industrial, scientific and military power in the world, and showed clear signs of moving to overtake the US in all these areas. This was despite the devastating losses it suffered while defeating the fascist powers of Germany, Romania, Hungary, and Bulgaria. The various peoples of the USSR were unified. Starvation and illiteracy were unknown throughout the country. Agriculture was completely collectivized and extremely productive. Preventive health care was the finest in the world, and medical treatment of exceptionally high quality was available free to all citizens. Education at all levels was free. More books were published in the USSR than in any other country. There was no unemployment.

4 From the obituary in *The Guardian* newspaper published in England on 6 March 1953:

Stalin transformed Russia from a backward country into one of the two greatest Powers in the world, with its industrial and intellectual resources multiplied many times over. He brought it safely through a terrible war. It is hard to say whether the same result could be achieved at less cost. But the cost was certainly exorbitant....

5 *Isaac Deutscher*, historian and Stalin's biographer, writing in the same newspaper:

Lenin had denied freedom to the old ruling classes and their parties. But he hoped that the working classes would enjoy the fullest economic and social liberty in the new State....
Stalin moulded that State into an autocracy.

autocracy   rule by one man

Questions

1 Why do you think that Svetlana, in 1967, gives such a sympathetic impression of her father and yet denounces him two years later?
2 Which sentences show that the statements of Khruschev, Franklin and *The Guardian* are written from particular points of view?
3 What criticisms do all the extracts, with the exception of Franklin's, make of Stalin?
4 From all the work you have done on Stalin, would you agree with his critics? Give reasons for your answer.
5 What strengths did Stalin have, according to Franklin and *The Guardian*?
6 Consider all the evidence, and write your own account: 'Joseph Stalin: an assessment'.

INDEX